ENTREPRENEURSHIP DEVELOPMENT AND PLANNING

INCULCATING SKILLS AND SPIRIT AMONG THE STUDENTS

DR. MUKTA GOYAL

Made with ❤ on the Notion Press Platform
www.notionpress.com

Contents

Preface

An entrepreneur is an individual who creates a new business, bearing most of the risks and enjoying most of the rewards. The process of setting up a business is known as entrepreneurship. Entrepreneurship that proves to be successful in taking on the risks of creating a start-up is rewarded with profits, fame, and continued growth opportunities. Entrepreneurship that fails results in losses and less prevalence in the markets for those involved.

Entrepreneurs are their own bosses. They make the decisions. They choose whom to do business with and what work they will do. They decide what hours to work, as well as what to pay and whether to take vacations. For many entrepreneurs the freedom to control their destiny is enough to outweigh the potential risks.

Entrepreneurship creates an opportunity for a person to make a contribution. Most new entrepreneurs help the local economy. A few—through their innovations—contribute to society as a whole.

This book helps the students to understand the concept of Entrepreneurship and the importance of small scale businesses . This book also highlights the government initiatives for MSMEs.

Dr. Mukta Goyal

ONE

FOUNDATION OF ENTREPRENEURSHIP

What is an Entrepreneur?

An entrepreneur is an individual who creates a new business, bearing most of the risks and enjoying most of the rewards. The process of setting up a business is known as entrepreneurship. The entrepreneur is commonly seen as an innovator, a source of new ideas, goods, services, and business/or procedures.

Entrepreneurs play a key role in any economy, using the skills and initiative necessary to anticipate needs and bringing good new ideas to market. Entrepreneurship that proves to be successful in taking on the risks of creating a start-up is rewarded with profits, fame, and continued growth opportunities. Entrepreneurship that fails results in losses and less prevalence in the markets for those involved.

Benefits of Entrepreneurship

i.Entrepreneurs provide job opportunities

One of the main reasons why individuals tend to become entrepreneurs is because they are unable to find suitable jobs. Entrepreneurs create new businesses and in turn create opportunities of employment for people. Many people have been made redundant due to COVID-19, thus starting a business is an opportunity to either work for themselves or they can help support and develop an entrepreneur's business. Not only are entrepreneurs able to generate an income for themselves but they also employ other individuals in their business operations. Therefore, people who did not have a job before will have a chance to have a career.

ii. Entrepreneurs increase competition & boost productivity

Entrepreneurs challenge existing firms to become more competitive as they often enter the market with lower prices and greater product variety. This can cause existing players in the market to re-assess their operations, increase their value, lower costs, and become more efficient.

Increased competition in an economy is advantageous because firms and individuals will source methods to better improve their operations. The new business formation of entrepreneurs with high-growth ambitions and innovation will push established firms to increase their productivity and enhance their performance.

iii. Entrepreneurs create a new businesses & new markets

As the trends in the world continue to change, people's demands will change, giving entrepreneurs an opportunity to start new businesses.

If a marketplace is saturated, this can result in entrepreneurs seeking new markets for their services and products, which can be considered as a positive impact on the economy. Entrepreneurs may even create entirely new industries that become the engines of future growth.

iv. Entrepreneurs add national income

The new products or services created by entrepreneurs result in new wealth from the new markets. Additionally, higher earnings due to entrepreneurship can help boost national income. This is in the form of higher government spending and tax revenue, resulting in investment in struggling sectors and human capital.

v. Entrepreneurs introduce innovative technologies

Individuals often resort to entrepreneurship to provide niche solutions or to use their creativity, technological knowledge, or finances to generate their own income. Innovative ideas and inventiveness are foundational driving factors for entrepreneurs which result in great contribution to the economy.

Like some of the legendary names in business, Bill Gates (Microsoft), Larry Ellison (Oracle), Steve Jobs (Apple) and many more, entrepreneurs create innovations. New and improved products enable new markets which often lead to economic growth.

Power of small business

The SBA defines a small business as any for-profit organization with fewer than 500 employees. There are small businesses in every industry sector. The majority of small businesses are self-employed individuals; these firms are classified as non-employers as they have no other paid employees.

Many Small Businesses Are Not Young Businesses

One-fourth of all small businesses are more than 20 years old. Nonemployee businesses tend to be younger, on average than other small businesses.

Many small businesses are owned by minorities:

Women-owned: 9.9 million businesses with $1.4 trillion in annual receipts Black or African-owned: 2.6 million businesses with $150 billion in annual receipts Veteran-owned: 2.5 million businesses with $1.4 trillion in annual receipts Hispanic-owned: 3.3 million businesses with $474 billion in annual receipts Asian-owned: 1.9 million businesses with $700 billion in annual receipts American Indian and Alaska Native-owned: 272,000 businesses with $39 billion in annual receipts

i. **Finance**

The inadequacy of funds to funnel in the operations of a small business prove to be a major hindrance to the development of the small business. Small businesses lack the creditworthiness needed in the capital market. Small businesses have poor creditworthiness.

The banks and industrial investors need collateral security, due to most of the small businesses being operated in the rural and semi-urban areas, these businesses lack collateral security to get finance for their business.

ii. **Raw Material**

For production purposes, businesses need raw materials. To get some output, they need to give some input. The quality of the raw material completely depends upon the quality of the input. But due to a tight budget, these businesses are unable to get good-quality raw materials for their production.

Bargaining power is non-existent because of the small number of purchases. Another issue linked here is the shortage of storage facilities, because of the shortage of storage facilities production needs to be quick and the sale good. This puts a heavy strain on these small businesses to sell their stock as quickly as possible.

iii. Managerial Skills

The operations of small businesses are carried out by a limited number of employees. This means that a single person usually manages the operations. The pressure on this manager is immense to satisfy the demands of production. Also, the manager might lack the managerial skills required to operate a unit.

iv. Skilled labour

Due to a shortage of funds, small businesses are unable to hire the proper candidate for the job. Also, they are not in a position to give high wages to the employees. This results in a drop in productivity per employee and the rate of labour are high. This proves to be a major obstruction in the operations of production.

v. Marketing

Marketing is one of the most important links to sell whatever the business plan to or has produced. Without marketing these businesses will not be able to achieve their goal of sales they planned. Direct marketing is not possible due to the lack of necessary infrastructure.

The shortage of finance does not let the business hire a good middleman. These middlemen exploit these businesses by paying low prices and delaying payments.

Case Study on Entrepreneurs

1.

Patricia Narayan –From selling tea on Marina Beach to running a chain of restaurants.

Back in the time, women were confined to their kitchens by societies. Today the world is modernizing and no doubt society's mindset has also changed. Nowadays, women are moving ahead by taking on new changeling work. if you see the entrepreneurial sector, they are also surprising across the world. Today I have brought up a woman entrepreneur story who faced a major issue in the past and now she is the **director of Sandeepha Chain restaurants**. I'm sure her story will inspire men and women who wish to full fill their dreams.

Source: https://images.app.goo.gl/54uHtGGwYSj4wa4R6

Her journey

Patricia Narayan was the firstborn baby in her family and she belonged to a very conservative family. She really has a great life with her siblings. Her bad time begins when she was nineteen, earlier younger age she fell in love with a man and got married. but her marriage went wrong. She said in TEDx, **"my marriage was a disaster I had committed the mistake."** Since she got married without asking permission from the family, her parents and in-law's family didn't want to accept her. She mentioned that **"I had brought myself and had nobody else to blame."** In such kind of situation, she had to take call do or die. She was a pregnant woman which made her change her priority she made a decision to live life for the child. Her journey was about to be tough because she had no financial source.

A 19 years woman had no prior work experience in any sector. She realized that nobody is going to give her a job. So, she pursued her passion of cooking and started a small business from home. initially, she was selling jam and squash and pickle. Fortunately, her first business went well. However, she was not able to produce enough products because she didn't have a commercial kitchen. Now she had a big concern about the next steps so she met with her father's friends who gave it to her kiosk. She decided to start a business alongside the marina beach in Chennai. But she did not know that she should have permission from the government to set up a kiosk at the beach. She went to the **PWD department** with her 1 and half year child. The PWD department secretary won't allow her to meet the seniors because Patricia didn't have any recommendations later. She said, "I started going every day just keeping in mind that one-day any senior will ask who is this lady, it did happen." One day she got permission to meet a senior. However, PWD's seniors took a year to get the work done. After all, Patricia Narayan started the business with a kiosk at the beach. In the kiosk, she made an agreement of many foods such as Samosa, cutlet, and French fries. But the first day she just sold one cup of coffee at the price 50 paise. She came home with heartbreak and had no courage to go kiosk the next day. At the time her mom motivated her and brought hope in mind. The next day she got up and went to the kiosk to sell the food. luckily the day didn't come again in her life.

She said **"people always asked me what is your qualification I proudly say that I have done MBA from Kiosk at the marina. I have learned all the business skills at the place."** She had an evening job at the marina beach. So, she started hunting the opportunity of another catering contract. She was taking contracts like bank catering, government catering and many more. She got one big breakthrough, when she got a catering contract from the national institute of port management, she was serving around 2000 people per day. After the time she never looked back. in her life, everything was going well but suddenly a bad thing happened, her daughter and son-in-law met with an accident and she lost both of them. At the time she felt everything is the end. Patricia Narayan pulled out herself and started working with her son. Later Patricia Narayan and her son started the restaurant and named the restaurant Sandeepha which was the name of her daughter. In 2010, she got a FICCI Woman entrepreneur award.

Life Lessons

- Always stick to what you know.

- Believe in yourself and the product you are making.

- Never compromise on quality.

- Never lose your self-confidence.

- You should know what you ask your employee to do.

- Struggle makes you even more mature to retain success for a long time.

- Success isn't a status or possession that stays with you for lifetime or a permanent stoppage of an accomplishment, it is rather a constant journey where you have to maintain your consistency.

- Pain is an inevitable part of life and it shouldn't stop us from moving forward as – 'moving is life' and 'still is dead'.

- To be a successful entrepreneur, you don't have to be highly educated (as degree doesn't always ensure success).

Achievements

- Initially started with 2 people, presently 200 people working in her restaurant.
- This is the journey from 50 paise a day to Rs 2 lakhs a day in 2014.
- Owns a chain of 14 restaurants.
- The journey from a life full of struggle and miseries to a life of success.
- From travelling in a cycle rickshaw to an auto rickshaw and now having her own car.

2.

The Success Story of Karsanbhai Patel, The Man Behind Nirma Washing Powder

Source: https://images.app.goo.gl/nXbaicBUqT2qZyhU8

Highlights

- Karsanbhai Patel is one such example from Gujarat. He quit his full-time government job to follow his dream.
- The year 1969 was a turning point in Karsanbhai's career.
- Instead of mourning, he found out a way to bring his daughter back to life.
- The good quality and low price of the detergent made a remarkable journey from Karsanbhai 100sq ft backyard to the middle-class house in India for a great value.

Someone once said that business is in any Gujarati's blood, and this saying has been proven to be true many times. What's commendable is their willingness take on any kind of small job to make things happen even if it means going door-to-door selling their products.

Karsanbhai Patel is one such example from Gujarat. He quit his full-time government job to follow his dream. He is said to have gone door-to-door selling detergent on his bicycle thereby turning the company into a formidable group. Today, he is one of the richest businessmen from Gujarat with a net worth of $4.1 billion, according to *Forbes*.

Almost everyone who's spent their time on the TV screen in the '90s can't ever forget the lyrics and catchy jingle young girl in a spotless white frock in a Nirma commercial advertisement. But most of us didn't know the real reason for setting up one of the most popular detergent brands in India and a man who nurtured this brand like a daughter. Here's all you need to know about Karsanbhai Patel and the reason he set up the Nirma brand.

Who is Karsanbhai Patel?

In 1945, Karsanbhai Patel was born to a farmer's family in Ruppur, Gujarat and by the age of 21, he graduated in Chemistry. After graduation, Karsanbhai tried to do a regular job like his peers. Karsanbhai also worked as a lab technician in the New Cotton Mills belonging to the Lalbhai Group. Following this brief stint, he even took up a job at the Geology and Mining Department of the Gujarat government.

How did Karsanbhai Patel invent Nirma detergent?

The year 1969 was a turning point in Karsanbhai's career, when a small farmer's son and a qualified Science graduate, Karsanbhai Patel, was trying to mix Soda Ash and a few ingredients to make detergent produce. One fine day, he got the formula right and it was then that he started producing detergents in the 100sq ft backyard of his home as an after-office business.

The accident that changed his life

Everything was going well in Karsan Bhai's life, but when Karsanbhai lost his daughter in a car accident his life almost changed. Instead of mourning, he found out a way to bring his daughter back to life. Only a few people knew of his daughter when she was alive, but it was this man's sheer determination and willpower that made his daughter famous throughout the country, even though she was no more.

A journey from 100sq ft backyard to every middle-class house

A one-man company, Karsanbhai would cycle through the neighbourhoods selling handmade detergent packets door to door at a price of Rs 3 per kg, (one-third the price of leading detergent brands) and it was his instant success *Mantra*. Karsanbhai branded his detergent soap, Nirma, after the name of his daughter. The good quality and low price of the detergent made a remarkable journey from Karsanbhai's 100sq ft backyard to the middle-class house in India for a great value. Fuelled by housewife-friendly advertisement jingles, Nirma revolutionized the detergent market, creating an entirely new segment in the market for detergent powder. At the time, detergent and soap manufacture was dominated by multinational corporations with products like Surf by Hindustan Lever, priced around Rs. 13 per kg.

Love of a father for his daughter

The product was close to Karsanbhai's heart and so he decided to name it 'Nirma'- the nickname of his lost daughter Nirupama. He also put her illustration (girl in the white frock) on the pack and TV commercials just to make sure that everybody remembers her. Such was the love of a father for his daughter. As for Nirma, it still remains among India's preferred choice of detergents. And its jingles will forever be etched in our memories.

Nirma University

In 1995, Karsanbhai Patel gave a different identity to Nirma when he founded the Nirma Institute of Technology in Ahmedabad. Thereafter, in April 2003, Nirma University was established by the first three institutions, under a special act passed by the Gujarat State Legislative Assembly.

According to Forbes, in the year 2004 Nirma's annual sales were as high as 8,00,000 tonnes. Karsanbhai Patel, who started his surf company from his home, is today 775th on the list of Billionaires of the world and 39th in the list of richest people in India. Currently, his net worth is $4.1 billion, according to *Forbes*.

Now, Karsanbhai Patel has handed over his successful business in hands of his two sons Rakesh Patel and Hirenbhai Patel. In 2010, he was awarded Padma Shri by Pratibha Patil, former President of India. Even today, Nirma remains the largest producer of soda ash in the world and the company has gone private since 2012.

Achievements

1. He has served twice as Chairman of the Development Council for Oils, Soaps and Detergents.
2. Patel has been conferred with Padma Shri Award for the year 2010.
3. The award was formally conferred by the President of India Mrs Pratibha Patil.
4. It was also announced on 7 June 2013 that he bought 400 million six-seater choppers.

5. The Gujarat Chamber of Commerce felicitated him as an "Outstanding Industrialist of the Eighties".
6. In 2009, he was ranked #92 by Forbes magazine, for the list of India's Richest businessmen

3. *The rags to riches story of Billionaire Ramesh Babu Barber*

v.

Ramesh Babu

Much of Ramesh Babu's early life was spent in a struggle for survival. Now, ensconced in the lap of success, he remains true to the vocation of his heart- a barber. Babu took up to sniping locks in high school, a profession he inherited from his father, to keep his family afloat. It is one that, even now, he does with great aplomb. He charges only a hundred rupees for his services. He has been featured in television channels and newspapers all over the country. His phenomenal success coupled with his disarming humility has earned him the moniker, 'Millionaire Barber'. It is the title he used while giving a TED talk earlier this year. This has made him something of an urban legend. Here Ramesh Babu, the Millionaire Barber, shares his utterly inspiring story.

Difficult Beginnings

I was born in a poor family. My father was a barber. He passed away in 1979 when I was just seven years old. My mother started working as a maidservant to make ends meet. My father had left behind a saloon business on Brigade road which my uncle took to running. He would give us five rupees a day from that. Five rupees, even in those days a pittance, was too less to see to me and my brother and sister's physical and educational needs. We took to having one meal a day just so we could survive. From when I was in middle school, I took up various odd jobs to make a little extra cash. I would deliver newspapers and milk bottles and whatever else was convenient to ease my mother's load a bit. This way I somehow managed to finish my tenth standard and joined evening PUC.

Breaking Point

Sometime in the nineties, when I was in my first PU, my mother had a bitter fight with my uncle. He had simply stopped paying us any money. I told her I should take over the saloon and run it myself. She was adamant that I prioritise my education, but I started working at the saloon too and learning the ropes of the business. In the mornings, I would be at the saloon and evenings at college. Then again at night, I would return to the saloon, which would remain open till 1 in the morning. Since then, I have been called a barber.

Breakthrough Idea

Later in 1993, I bought a used Maruti van. My uncle had bought a small car and petty pride made me buy one too. I pooled my tiny savings, took a loan and felt a grim satisfaction at having bought a marginally grander vehicle than him. My grandfather had to mortgage his property to enable the loan. The loan interest was six thousand and eight hundred rupees and I was reeling from having to make the payments.

The lady whose house my mother used to work, Nandini Akka as I like to call her, asked me why I don't rent out the car instead of it just lying around. She taught me the basics of doing this kind of business. She became like a sister to me and remains a big part of my life even today. She called me to her daughter's wedding and showed me off!

Building a successful business

From 1994 onward I seriously got into the car rental business. The first company I rented it out to was Intel because that's where Nandini Akka was working and she helped arrange it. Gradually, I started adding more cars to the fleet. Till 2004, I only had about five to six cars. I was focused on getting the saloon business off the ground, so this was not my priority. The business was not doing well as the competition at this level was intense. Everyone had small cars. I thought of getting into luxury cars because that is something that no one else was doing.

Rolls Royce_Barber

On Taking Risks

When I was buying my first luxury car, in 2004, everyone told me that I was making a big mistake. Forty lakhs in 2004 for a car, even a luxury car, was a very big deal. I was extremely apprehensive but simply had to take the chance. I told myself that I would sell off the car if worse came to worst. Fortunately for me, the risk paid off remarkably. No other car rental service had luxury cars of this stature. There were ones who had purchased second-hand models and the conditions of those cars were far from pristine. I was the first person in Bangalore to invest in a brand-new luxury car and it did very well.

If you want to do business, you must be willing to take risks. When I bought my Rolls Royce in 2011, people warned me about the scope of failures against buying such a tremendously expensive car. I told myself that I had taken a risk in 2004, so why can't I take one again almost a decade later? It cost me almost four crore rupees, to buy the car. But once again, it was a risk that paid off. It's been three years since, and it's has proven to be tremendously popular. In December this year, the EMI payments will be over.

Biggest Challenges

Every business will face challenges and pitfalls. Last April, I had to pay over three crores in road taxes alone. I still don't know how I managed to pull the amount together. I borrowed from so many people and put up property documents to get the cash. Every business will have recurring formidable challenges. The idea is to embrace them wholeheartedly and tackle them vehemently. I had been in the red for a while with the road tax, but in another year or so we will be free of that.

Ideas for the Future

Earlier we used to pay taxes quarterly. As of now, I have had to put a hold on the plans for expansion because the taxes have become sky-high. In 2015 we are going to buy some stretch limousines and other such vehicles.

Message to Aspiring Entrepreneurs

Ramesh Babu reiterated the simple message to entrepreneurs that he told students to follow in his TED talk.

He still goes to his barber shop every day as he doesn't want to lose touch with his roots. "Every morning at 6, I go to the garage to check on the business. Then, by 10.30 I'm in the office. And every evening, without fail, by 5.30 I'm at our salon. There are also people who specially come in to get haircuts from me. I have a loyal client base from Kolkata and Mumbai as well," he says.

Ramesh is also teaching the skill of hairstyling to his kids, two daughters and one son. "It's a skilled job and they'll have to learn about it. I take them with me to the shop sometimes, but they are too young to take on anything now. Till I'm there, and hopefully even after, I'll make sure the salon is running successfully. I take no offs, unless it's for a family trip. I have always believed that work is worship. Inner Space is where my bread and butter comes from."

Even today, being such a rich man, he did not forget his roots. He cuts the hair of his regular customers for just Rs 65.

Babu owes his success to doing what he thought was best. "Whatever I did, I did well, that's all I can say," he smiles.

Achievements

Ramesh Babu started his business in 1994 and is Now a Billionaire. **He got more than 75 luxury cars on his fleet – owns more than 400 cars, including a Maybach S600, BMW, Audi, and Rolls Royce**

4. Dhirubhai Ambani – The Founder of Reliance

Source: The CEO story

Dhirubhai Ambani was born on 28 Dec. 1932 as the third son to a school teacher in Gujarat with moderate means. Ambani moved to Aden, Yemen when he was 16 for a livelihood. He started his career as a dispatch clerk before becoming the distributor for Shell Products. He was later promoted as a manager in an oil filling station at the port of Aden.

The Yemeni Rial Coin had high content of pure silver in those days. Young Dhirubhai perceived high demand for 'rial' in London Stock Exchange and purchased them in bulk and melted the coins in silver and sold it to bullion traders in London. Though it was stopped in 3 months, D.A. made a few lakhs of Rupees in this transaction.

D.A. returned to India after 10 years and found Reliance Commercial Company with a capital of Rs.15000/= in Masjid Bunder in Mumbai in a 350 Sq.ft. space with one telephone, one table, three chairs and with a business mission of importing polyester yarn and exporting spices.. He went on to establish Reliance Textiles in 1964 under the brand name "Vimal" and the World Bank applauded the brand as the best Polyester Cloth. Perceiving success, Dhirubhai established Reliance IndustriesLtd in 1970s.

Dhirubhai Ambani is credited with starting the equity cult in India. More than 58,000 investors from various parts of India subscribed to Reliance's

IPO in 1977. Dhirubhai was able to convince people of rural Gujarat that being shareholders of his company will only bring returns to their investment.

RIL holds the distinction that it is the only Public Limited Company whose several Annual General Meetings were held in stadiums.In 1986, The Annual General Meeting of Reliance Industries was held in Cross Maidan, Mumbai, was attended by more than 30,000 shareholders.

Dhirubhai Ambani's takes control of the Mumbai Stock exchange : In 1982, RIL was coming out with a rights issue of the partly convertible debenture and it was rumoured that the objective was not to get the then-existing stock price to slide by an inch. A group of stock brokers in Calcutta joined together as a Bear Cartel. Taking this as an opportunity they started to short-sell RIL scrips. Friends of RIL counteracted this move and the Bulls started buying the scrips on the Bombay Stock Exchange. The bulls kept on buying and a price of Rs. 152 per share was maintained till the day of settlement. The Bear Cartel believed that the Bulls would accept settlement under the then-prevalent " Badla " system. On the day of settlement, the Bear Cartel was taken aback when the Bulls demanded physical delivery of shares. To complete the transaction the much-needed cash was provided to the stock brokers who had brought shares of Reliance by none other than Dhirubhai Ambani. In case of non-settlement, the Bulls demanded an 'Unbadala' (penalty sum) of Rs.35 per share. With this, the demand increased and the shares of Reliance shot above 180 rupees in minutes. The settlement caused an enormous uproar in the market and Dhirubhai Ambani was the unquestioned king of the stock markets.

The situation was completely out of control. Authorities of the Bombay Stock exchange intervened in the matter and brought down the "Unbadla" rate to Rs. 2 with a stipulation that the Bear Cartel has to give the delivery of shares within few days. The Bear Cartel brought shares of Reliance from the market at higher price levels and it was also realized that Dhirubhai Ambani himself supplied those shares to the Bear Cartel and earned a healthy profit out of The Bear Cartel's adventure.

After this incident, many questions were raised by his detractors and the press. Not many people were able to understand how a yarn trader till a few years ago was able to get in so much cash flow during the crisis. RBI was called upon to investigate the matter. It was clarified by RBI that the money flow into RIL was due to Rs.220 million investment made by NRIs thru' various Companies like 'crocodiles etc. and that there was nothing unethical nor illegal in the whole matter.

A film inspired by the life of Dhirubhai is set to release in January 2007. The Hindi Film Guru, directed by ManiRathnam and with music by Rahman will show the struggle of a man who strives to make his mark in life. The movie stars Abhishek Bachan and Aishwarya Rai in leading roles.

Achievements

A book was believed to be written on Dhirubhai Ambani by Hamish McDonald in the late 1980s, however, the unauthorized biography of Ambani was not published in India. The author is said to have covered Dhirubhai Ambani's business and all political conquest in his book. It is also believed that a Hindi film, Guru is loosely inspired by the life of Dhirubhai Ambani. The movie was released in 2007 and highlights the struggle of an individual who tries to make his mark. However, nothing was officially confirmed about it.

Dhirubhai Ambani was a highly accomplished professional and during the course of his life, he has had many achievements and awards. Here are some of his accomplishments:

1. In the year 1996 Dhirubhai Ambani was featured among the "Power 50-the most powerful people in Asia" by Asiaweek magazine.
2. In the years 1998 and 2000 Dhirubhai Ambani was once again featured among the "Power 50-the most powerful people in Asia".
3. On June 15, 1998, Dhirubhai Ambani was awarded a Dean's Medal by The Wharton School, University of Pennsylvania. The Dean's Medal was to honour the example set by Dhirubhai Ambani for being an outstanding leader. He was also the first Indian to win a Dean's Medal.
4. Dhirubhai Ambani was conferred with the honour of "Man of the Century" in November 2000 in Mumbai. The award was conferred by Chemtech Foundation and Chemical Engineering World for making an outstanding contribution to the Chemical industry in India.
5. In August 2001, Dhirubhai Ambani also won The Economic Times Award for Corporate Excellence.
6. The federation of Indian Chambers of Commerce and Industry named Dhirubhai Ambani as Man of the 20th Century.
7. A postal stamp was released by India Post on 28th December 2002 featuring Dhirubhai Ambani.
8. In Oct 2011, Dhirubhai Ambani was posthumously awarded the ABLF Global Asian Award at the Asian Business Leadership Forum Awards.

5. *Kailash Katkar – Founder and CEO of Quick Heal Technologies LTD*

Whizsky

Kailash Katkar is the Managing Director and Chief Executive Officer of the leading IT security solutions provider, **Quick Heal Technologies.** It is a 28-year-old company providing Anti-Virus solutions based in India. Kailash also initiated a series of awareness workshops named "**Rotary Cyber Safety Initiative**"by bringing together cybersecurity experts, law enforcement authorities, and academicians on a single platform. The main objective of this initiative is to focus on Internet safety for kids and teenagers.

Early Life

Kailash was born in a small village named Rahmitapur in Maharashtra to a typical Maharashtrian family. Later his family moved to Pune and his father used to work at Philips as a machine setter. Kailash has two siblings Sanjay and Asha.

Kailash flunked his ninth standard and dropped out of school and took up a job at a local radio and calculator repair shop. Although his brother,

Sanjay completed class 10th, electronics fascinated him and he decided to pursue his engineering in electronics. Kailash encouraged Sanjay to study computers and the latter finished his Bachelor's in Computer Science from Modern College, Pune.

In 1990 he started his own repair shop along with a seed capital of Rs. 15,000 from his savings. That was the first step in his entrepreneurial journey. Alongside he began upgrading his skill set and began reading and attending short computer courses which eventually laid the foundation for Quick Heal.

Quick Heal's Foundation

In 1993 alongside his calculator repair shop, Kailash started his new venture called **CAT Computer Services** with an office based in a small one-room electrical device repair station. Within a few months of starting his new venture, he also managed to break into the corporate world by winning the annual maintenance contract for **New India Insurance.**

During this process, Kailash managed to see a future issue evolving which is computer viruses. Since the internet was becoming popular, it only meant that the computers would be at great risk and would create multiple channels for viruses to reach the machines. That is when he began working on a definite solution for the same.

By this time his brother Sanjay who was studying Computer Engineering in Pune had begun writing software programs and he insisted Sanjay start developing a basic model of antivirus software for his own firm CAT Computer Services. That is how the antivirus Quick Heal came into existence.

The Growth Story of Quick Heal

In 1994, the first Quick Heal anti-virus for DOS was released followed by Win 3.1 in 1995 and Windows 95 in 1996 as well and it was well accepted by the market. At that time the duo was offering their product to other vendors for a fee of Rs. 700 which was the cheapest among his competitors.

Since then there has been no looking back for the company. Some of the major developments made by the company to date are mentioned below-

- The company launched its own website www.quickheal.com in 1998.
- In 2002 company saw immense growth in business and bought an office space of 2,000 sq ft in Pune for Rs. 25 lakhs.
- Between 2006 to 2010 Quick Heal signed a deal with Microsoft for bundling of Quick Heal anti-virus with Genuine Windows XP.

Today the company has more than 12000 employees with more than 17 million customers across 112+ countries has transformed into a globally-known brand.

Awards and Recognitions

- Entrepreneurs International Honors
- Maxell Award for Maharashtra Corporate Excellence 2012
- 2012 Brands Academy 'Entrepreneur of the Year in IT Security
- Deloitte Fast 50 award
- Red Herring Asia Award

TWO

Launching Entrepreneurial Ventures

Creativity and Innovation in Entrepreneurship

Creativity is thinking new ideas and innovation is doing new things.

Creativity is the ability to develop new ideas and to discover new ways of looking at problems and opportunities.

Innovation is the ability to apply creative solutions to those problems and opportunities in order to enhance people's lives or to enrich society.

Entrepreneurship = Creativity + Innovation

CREATIVITY

Creativity is when people use their imagination to create new ideas, solve problems and think of possibilities that no one else has thought of before. The scope of creativity is limited only by one's ability to think outside the norm. The nature of creativity means that an idea's creation is unique and original to the creative thinker. Creativity is not a genetic trait, but something that a person develops as they continue to learn and grow and use their imagination for various forms of expression. Creativity has no inherent value unless a person manifests it into reality.

STEPS IN THE CREATIVE PROCESS

1. Opportunity or Problem Recognition: A person discovers that a new opportunity exists or a problem needs resolution.

2. Immersion: The individual concentrates on the problem and becomes immersion it. He or she will recall and collect information that seems

relevant, dreaming up alternatives without refining or evaluating them,

3. Incubation: The person keeps the assembled information in mind for a while. He or she does not appear to be working on the problem actively; however, the Subconscious mind is still engaged. While the information is simmering it is Being arranged into meaningful new patterns.

4. Insight: The problem-conquering solution flashes into the person's mind at an unexpected time, such as on the verge of sleep, during a shower, or while Running, Insight is also called the Aha! Or Eureka! Experience.

5. Verification and Application: The individual sets out to prove that the creative solution has merit. Verification procedures include gathering supporting evidence, using logical persuasion, and experimenting with new ideas.

INNOVATION

Innovation is the process of taking creative ideas and exploiting their benefit for commercial and financial success. Innovation is the creation of an innovator. Since innovation is the application of creative ideas, it's innately connected to creativity and they both work in tandem with one another. Innovation can be a physical object and a concept to improve or create a new process. People innovate to solve a problem or make society functionally more convenient.

TYPES OF INNOVATIONS

There are four distinct types of innovation, these are as follows:

- **The invention** is described as the creation of a new product, service or process. Something that has not been tried before.
- **Extension** - The expansion of an existing product, service or process. This would mean that the entrepreneur takes an existing idea and applies it differently.
- **Duplication** - Copying (replicating) an existing product or service and then adding the entrepreneur's own creative touch. order to improve it.
- **Synthesis** - A combination of more than one existing product or service into a new product, or service. This means that several different ideas are combined into one new product or service.

THE INNOVATION PROCESS

1. Analytical planning Carefully identifying the product or service features, design as well as resources that will be needed.

2. Resource organization Obtaining the required resources, materials, technology, and human or capital resources.

3. Implementation - Applying the resources in order to accomplish the plans

4. Commercial application The provision of value to customers, reward employees, and satisfy the stakeholders,

Methods to initiate ventures

Outline your main goal

What is your objective? Are you focusing on a problem or a solution? If you're focusing on only developing a solution, then you will fail. Why? Because a customer will only buy if they think you will solve their problem. The business world is littered with great products that failed, or needed someone else to make it a viable businesses (look up the origin stories of Starbucks or Mcdonald's).

That brings me to an important point that investors want to hear– can your business model scale? Have you thought about the future- as any investor would want multiplying returns? So keep it simple and scalable.

· **Outline your values**

At what cost are you willing to do business, or better still, what values will govern how you will do business? You might think this is not necessary to know for a young startup, but it is very crucial. When you hit the ground running (and you will be!), most of your time is spent on crises that never stop, and on staging meetings with current and future investors, customers, suppliers and distributors. As a result, newer employees joining the company may not know the principles and values that you run the business with, and perhaps take for granted.

· **Build a product concept that works**

A lot of investor money does go into research and development and concept ideas –see Elon Musk's SpaceX or Tesla- but in the end, the market only accepts products that work. You need proof of concept, and it needs to be able to scale quickly without too many bugs (like Sarah Blakely's Spanx), or you need a heavyweight investor or celebrity endorser who has the connections and clout to help you get the help you need.

· **Find a market that appreciates your product**

While it's tempting to want your product to be the next instant global brand, you need to remember to start small. Start in markets you can win –which are often the markets where guard. Jamalon is a great example– it is now the largest Arabic online bookstore.

· **Map your networks**

If you haven't done this yet- start now, seriously! Networks are assets that are nurtured and developed. Build your networks methodologically. Figure out who you want to meet and why, and then arrange to meet them. Classmates, employees and customers can bring in strong networks– not just investors. Create an advisory board, and this is an opportunity to rope in some key mentors. Research shows internationally diversified networks leads to more funding, more customers and more expert knowledge that you can't pay for in your early years.

· **Outline key indicators of performance**

Sure, you measure customer acquisition numbers, sales and profits- these are all common fundamentals, but don't forget to look at customer retention, return on investments and referrals as well. Understand the beating pulse of your business so you can predict the slumps. More importantly, when chasing capital or employees, remember at what cost you give away your share of your company. Whether customer, supplier, distributor, employee or investor, read the fine print.

· **Provide value to your stakeholders**

Ask yourself what value you provide to each of your key stakeholders. Start with employees, customers, suppliers, distributors, shareholders and even mentors. Here's a simple logic to keep in mind: if the cost of being with you is more than the benefit, then people will walk away. Invest time to make sure you keep your value stakeholders close.

· **Be careful about what you promise**

You can't control the media, so be careful with what you promise. Too much media exposure can open you up to close scrutiny, and worse, highlight every inaccurate statement you made unwittingly, even in good faith.

Legal challenges in Entrepreneurship ventures

1. Incorrect Formation of a Company based on the type of Entity

Whenever you start your own business you are always worried about one thing i.e., Legal Registration and Documentation. The type of business selected has an influence on the funding options for the company, its tax responsibilities, and the personal liability of the owners. The right format can help save taxes as well as protect the personal assets of the proprietors in times of crisis. There are 5 categories of Legal Entity for business registration in India- 1. Sole Proprietorship Firm, 2. Partnership Firm, 3. Private Limited Company, 4. Limited Liability Partnership Firm (LLP), 5. One Person Company (OPC).

2. Not having a proper Co-Founder's Agreement

A co-founder's agreement lays down all the terms and conditions between the co-founders of a start-up regarding how the business will be operated. The co-founder's agreement is a written agreement which provides legal binding in case there is any dissonance between the co-founders.

3. Not doing proper due diligence before Fundraising

A start-up goes through various stages of fundraising, including Angel funding, Seed Round funding and Growth/Early-stage funding. After the Angel funding stage, start-ups go through further fundraising processes, after having executed a term sheet, which is legal due diligence.

4. Equity Distribution

Equity is ownership. Equity represents the percentage of ownership interest in a given company. There is no right way to divide equity and it depends on the situation of each start-up. For the investors investing in a start-up, Equity means the percentage of the company's shares that a start-up is willing to sell to investors for an amount of money.

5. Annual Compliance

The moment a start-up is incorporated, it is subjected to different statutory and regulatory compliances. A business registered in India is required to comply with the various annual legal compliances laid down by the Companies Act. Businesses. Registered companies are many times unable to keep track of their annual compliance requirements and fall under the scrutiny of the Ministry of Corporate Affairs (MCA).

LEGAL CHALLENGES IN ENTREPRENEURSHIP VENTURES

a) The Inception of an entrepreneurial venture is comprised of

1) Laws governing intellectual property: patents, copyrights, trademarks

2) Forms of business organization: sole proprietorship, partnership, corporation, franchise

3) Tax considerations

4) Capital formation

5) Liability questions

b) The Ongoing Venture is comprised of

1) Personnel law: hiring and firing policies, equal employment opportunity, collective bargaining

2) Contract law: legal contracts, sales contracts, leases

c) Growth and Continuity of the Venture is comprised of

1) Tax considerations: federal, state and local, payroll, incentives

2) Governmental regulations: property, administrative agencies, consumer law

3) Continuity of ownership rights: property laws and ownership, wills, trusts and ownership, bankruptcy.

I. **Incorrect Formation of a Company based on type of Entity**

Whenever you start your own business you are always worried with one thing i.e., Legal Registration and Documentation. The type of business selected has an influence on the funding options for the company, its tax responsibilities, and the personal liability of the owners. The right format can help save taxes as well as protect the personal assets of the proprietors in times of crisis. There are 5 categories of Legal Entity for business registration in India- 1. Sole Proprietorship Firm, 2. Partnership Firm, 3. Private Limited Company, 4. Limited Liability Partnership Firm (LLP), 5. One Person Company (OPC).

II. Not having a proper Co-Founder's Agreement

A co-founder's agreement lays down all the terms and conditions between the co-founders of a start-up regarding how the business will be operated. The co-founder's agreement is a written agreement which provides legal binding in case there is any dissonance between the co-founders.

III. Not doing proper due diligence before Fund raising

A start-up goes through various stages of fundraising, including Angel funding, Seed Round funding and Growth/Early-stage funding. After the Angel funding stage, start-ups go through further fundraising process, after having executed a term sheet, which is legal due diligence.

IV. Equity Distribution

Equity is ownership. Equity represents the percentage of ownership interest in a given company. There is no right way to divide equity and it depends on the situations of each start-up. For the investors investing in a start-up, Equity means the percentage of the company's shares that a start-up is willing to sell to investors for an amount of money.

V. Annual Compliance

The moment a start-up is incorporated, it is subjected to different statutory and regulatory compliances. A business registered in India is required to comply with the various annual legal compliances laid down by the Companies Act. Businesses. Registered as companies are many a times unable to keep track of their annual compliance requirements and fall under the scrutiny of the Ministry of Corporate Affairs (MCA).

Intended Learning Outcomes

1. Articulate the concept of intellectual property protection in the form of patents, copyrights and trademarks.
2. Identify the definitive characteristics of the legal structures for entrepreneurial ventures.
3. Identify the specific forms of partnerships and corporations

Intellectual Property Protection: Patents
a. Securing a Patent: Basic Rules
b. Securing a Patent: The Application
Intellectual Property Protection: Copyrights
a. Understanding Copyright Protection
b. Protecting Ideas
Intellectual Property Protection: Trademarks

a. Avoiding Trademark Pitfalls b. Trade Secrets

b. Trademark Protection on the Internet

Intellectual Property Protection: Patents

A patent provides the owner with exclusive rights to hold, transfer, and license the production and sale of the product or process. Design patents last for 14 years; all others last for 20 years. The patent provides the owner with a temporary monopoly on the innovation.

Securing a Patent: Basic Rules

Recommendations made by experts in pursuing a patent effectively:

Pursue patents that are broad, are commercially significant, and offer a strong position.

Prepare a patent plan in detail.

Have your patent relate to your original action plan.

Intellectual Property Protection: Copyrights

A copyright provides exclusive rights to creative individuals for the protection of their literary or artistic productions. Understanding Copyright Protection Copyright in tangible form Author's own work

Product of own skill or judgment Fair use" doctrine of copyrights-reproduction of a copyrighted work for purposes f criticism, comment, news reporting, teaching, scholarship, or research Protecting Ideas?

It is not possible to copyright an idea, but the particular mode of expression of that idea can be copyrighted.

Search for Entrepreneurial Capital

Venture capital firms differ in size, geographic focus, industry speciality, and funding stage. Most firms stay closely involved with their portfolio companies, taking board positions, recommending management candidates, providing advice, and identifying valuable contacts.

Entrepreneurs approaching venture capitalists must have a business plan; however, it should be short and concise, rather than presenting the business in full detail because venture capitalists will conduct exhaustive due diligence. The plan should spell out the amount of funding the entrepreneur is seeking but should not detail the terms.

· **The Founders**

Founders can obviously invest in their own company at any time. However, you usually see this happening when the company has just been founded. When a company is set up, in many cases, no revenues or external financing is available, yet there are always some startup costs to cover.

- **The 3Fs: family, friends and fools**

This type of financing is often pursued to cover the costs of setting up a new company or to bridge the gap to a first round of (pre-)seed funding. The advantage of this funding type is that it is a quick and cheap way of collecting cash, especially if you take into account the risk that the 3Fs take (which they are not always aware of themselves: hence, "fools").

Usually, the amounts concerned with this type of investment are not too high and are typically repaid as a loan (with or even without interest) or are invested in exchange for a small equity share in the company. When the invested amounts, share percentages and level of professionalism increase, then we speak of angel investing.

- **Angels/Informals**

Go for an angel if you are looking for seed funding within the abovementioned range. Angels typically offer "smart capital": not just money, but also networking opportunities and knowledge within specific sectors. Try to find an angel that fits with your company in terms of experience and sector knowledge.

- **Subsidies**

ALWAYS, and we can be very brief about this. Subsidies are relevant during almost every company stage, from startup to corporate, from freelancer to publicly traded company. As mentioned before, many subsidies only focus on a certain geographical area and, often, there is also a specific sector focus. Therefore, it is important to look for a subsidy that fits your company.

- **Venture capital/private equity**

Private equity is the collective name for professional investment firms that invest in companies that are not publicly listed. Venture capital (VC) is a type of private equity that focuses specifically on (from the investor's perspective) risky investments in early-stage companies.

Discuss in class ways to enhance the business in the most innovative manner:-

· **Think like an artist**

Back in 2013, fledgling cleantech startup Nanoleaf set out to make the world's most energy-efficient lightbulb. And it did. The problem was the lightbulb was too expensive and sales were poor. "We realized then that broader market appeal was the key to broader impact," says co-founder and CEO Jimmy Chu. So, brilliant aesthetics became key to Nanoleaf's strategy. Assembling a team of top-notch designers, the company ditched bulbs for technicolour, and LED wall panels that mimicked sunshine. These new devices could react to music and human touch, be programmed by phones and tablets and still maintain strong energy efficiency. Today, the company sells products in 45 countries, with offices in Toronto, Paris and Shenzhen, supporting everything from art installations to therapeutic practices. Chu explains his team's growth this way: "If you want to create something revolutionary, something people love, you have to think like an artist."

· **Give your team flexibility**

Studies routinely show that flex hours increase productivity and improve talent attraction and retention. Just ask Shonezi Noor, director of operations at Toronto-based Sampler. Noor had suffered a concussion before being hired, but the company's progressive HR policies allowed her to excel in her new role. When Noor had a physiotherapy appointment in the afternoon, she could start work earlier in the morning; if she was feeling light-headed, she could go home and make up the time later.

· **Hire non-human helpers**

Yes, it's time to talk about dogs. More than just walking hugs, canine coworkers reduce stress, invite physical activity and promote team bonding — all good ingredients for cooking up great ideas. Having dogs in-office also relieves workers of paying for expensive walkers and sitters. So, it's no surprise that startups like SoapBox (a software company that makes its bread on fostering meaningful employee interactions) enlist dog teammates to boost culture and draw hard-working humans.

- **Earn from people that aren't like you**

Nine days before the World Health Organization made an official statement about COVID-19, Toronto-based startup BlueDot had already alerted its clients about the novel virus spreading rapidly out of Wuhan. The company's incredible AI technology (informed by a seemingly bottomless reservoir of public health sources, moderated reports, news feeds, flight itineraries and other data) was built to predict such a crisis. But it wasn't built overnight. For seven years, founder and CEO Dr. Kamran Khan tirelessly assembled a diverse team of more than 50 experts to power and fine-tune the mind of his machine — doctors, data scientists, geographers, veterinarians, software developers, epidemiologists, etc.

- Articulate the conce
- Empathize with strangers

Entrepreneurs often come up with the best ideas when they have other people in mind. Vancouverites Stephen Ufford and Tanis Jorge had founded and sold three data-driven businesses earlier in their careers, and were looking for a way to create broader social good through tech. In 2011, they started their company Trulioo after watching a news segment wherein an Indian woman was moved to tears upon seeing her Facebook profile for the first time. You see, in the developing world, close to one billion people don't have an identity record, making it impossible for them to benefit from something as simple as a bank account.

- **Turn pain into purpose**

Entrepreneurial goodwill can also be born from trying to heal wounds from within. It was through great personal pain that Adam Blackman found renewed purpose as a businessperson. Already a physician and founder of a sleeping-clinic network, Blackman's world was turned upside-down when his 91-year-old grandmother, Rose, began having numerous health issues. In and out of the hospital, she quickly declined before dying in a nursing home. Devastated, Blackman made it his professional duty to better serve the elder population. "All people should have the right to age at home," he says. "I realized then that technology could and should play a bigger role." Today, Blackman is co-founder and CEO of Mavencare, a startup that provides personalized healthcare and specialty treatment for seniors. And elder care has never been so important. In Canada, the pandemic has ravaged long-term care homes, representing roughly 80 percent of all COVID-19-related deaths.

To be successful in sustainable business practices often requires entrepreneurship and innovation. This chapter provides an overview of entrepreneurship and innovation as it relates to sustainable business. The discussion is most relevant to sustainable businesses focused on offering new products and services in response to societal concerns. The importance of entrepreneurship and innovation also applies to companies that change how they produce products and services. The latter companies can use innovative practices and entrepreneurship to establish their brand name and to be market leaders in doing things that create shared value for society and their companies and also, over time, contribute to changes in practices in their industry.

THREE

FORMULATION OF THE ENTREPRENEURIAL PLAN

THE ASSESSMENT FUNCTION WITH OPPORTUNITIES

The term 'opportunity' also covers a product or project. Hence, the identification of an opportunity or a product or project is identical and, therefore, all these three terms are used as synonyms. The Government of India's "Look East Policy" through North East is an example of 'opportunity' to do business in items like tea, handicrafts, herbals, turmeric, etc.

In general sense, the term opportunity implies a good chance or a favourable situation to do something offered by circumstances. In the same vein, business opportunity means a good or favourable change available to run a specific business in a given environment at a given point of time.

The term 'opportunity' also covers a product or project. Hence, the identification of an opportunity or a product or project is identical and, therefore, all these three terms are used as synonyms. The Government of India's "Look East Policy" through North East is an example of 'opportunity' to do business in items like tea, handicrafts, herbals, turmeric, etc.

The processes at times create a situation, or say, dilemma resembling 'Hen or Egg' controversy. That is, at one point, the intending entrepreneur may find one product or project as an opportunity and may enchant and like it, but at the other moment may dislike and turn down it and may think for and find other product or project as an opportunity for him/her. This process of dilemma goes on for some intending entrepreneurs rendering them into the problem of what product or project to start. Then, how to overcome this problem of product identification and selection?

One way to overcome this dilemmatic situation is to know how the existing entrepreneurs identified the opportunity and set up their enterprises. An investigation into the historical experiences of Indian small enterprises in this regard reveals some interesting factors.

In its simplest form... A Business Plan is a **GUIDE**—a **ROADMAP** for your business that outlines goals and details how you plan to achieve those goals.

8 traits of successful entrepreneurs

Starting a business is a lot of work. Anyone who tells you it's not is either lying or has never actually started one themselves. The hours are long, sacrifices are great and you are assaulted with new problems and challenges every day with seemingly no end. If you don't have the constitution to weather these things, your business could implode on you faster than it started.

Clearly, entrepreneurship is not for everyone. But how do you know whether it's for you? You should start by asking yourself what it takes to be a leader because, for the most part, you'll be doing a lot of the work up front by yourself. If you can't lead yourself through start-up, chances are you won't likely be able to lead your business and future employees through growth and on to success.

If you enjoy only a few actual hours of real work per day, the rest of the time spent either looking busy or hanging out at the water cooler to catch up on TV talk, a modest but steady pay check and benefits and are okay with routine day-in and day-out, stop reading here and go back to your cushy desk job.

If you seek a challenge wrought with risk but with tremendous potential reward both financially and morally, read on friend, for you have something of what it takes to be a successful entrepreneur.

1. Strong leadership qualities

Leaders are born, not made. Do you find yourself being the go-to person most of the time? Do you find people asking your opinion or to help guide or make decisions for them? Have you been in management roles throughout your career? A leader is someone who values the goal over any unpleasantness the work it takes to get there may bring. But a leader is more than just tenacious. A leader has strong communication skills and the ability to amass a team of people toward a common goal in a way that the entire team is motivated and works effectively to get there as a team. A leader earns the trust and respect of his team by demonstrating positive work qualities and confidence, then fostering an environment that proliferates these values through the team. A leader who nobody will follow is not a leader of anything at all.

2. Highly self-motivated

You probably know from knowing even a little bit about some of the most famous business entrepreneurs in history that leaders are typically pretty intense personalities. Nobody makes progress by sitting back and waiting for it to find them. Successful people go out into the world and invoke change through their actions. Typically, leaders enjoy challenges and will work tirelessly to solve problems that confront them. They adapt well to changing situations without unravelling and are typically expert of helping their teams change with them by motivating them toward new goals and opportunities. Often you will learn that successful entrepreneurs are driven by a more complete vision or goal than simply the task at hand and able to think on a more universal level in that regard. They are also often very passionate about their ideas that drive toward these ultimate goals and are notoriously difficult to steer off the course.

3. Strong sense of basic ethics and integrity

Business is sustainable because there is a common, understood code of ethics universally that underpins the very fabric upon which commerce is conducted. While cheaters and thieves may win in the short term, they invariably lose out in the long run. You will find that successful, sustainable business people maintain the highest standards of integrity because, at the end of the day, if you cannot prove yourself a credible business person and nobody will do business with you, you are out of business. With importance in working with clients or leading a team, effective leaders admit to any error made and offer solutions to correct rather than lie about, blame others for, or dwell on the problem itself.

4. Willingness to fail

Successful entrepreneurs are risk takers who have all gotten over one very significant hurdle: they are not afraid of failure. That's not to say that they rush in with reckless abandon. In fact, entrepreneurs are often successful because they are calculating and able to make the best decisions in even the worst of cases. However, they also accept that, even if they make the best decision possible, things don't always go according to plan and may fail anyhow. If you've heard the old adage, "nothing ventured, nothing gained," that's exactly what it's saying: do not be afraid to fail, put it out there and give it your best shot. Again, there's not one successful entrepreneur out there sitting on his couch asking, "what if?"

5. Serial innovators

Entrepreneurs are almost defined by their drive to constantly develop new ideas and improve on existing processes. In fact, that's how most of them got into business in the first place. Successful people welcome change and often depend on it to improve their effectiveness as leaders and ultimately the success of their businesses as many business concepts relies on improving products, services and processes in order to win business.

6. Know what you don't know

While successful entrepreneurs are typically strong personalities overall, the best have learned that there's always a lesson to be learned. They are rarely afraid to ask questions when it means the answers will provide them insight they can then leverage to affect. Successful entrepreneurs are confident, but not egotistical to the point that their bull-headedness is a weakness that continually prohibits them from seeing a bigger picture and ultimately making the best decisions for the business.

7. Competitive spirit

Entrepreneurs enjoy a challenge and they like to win. They would have to since starting a business is pretty much one of the biggest challenges a person can take on in their lifetime. In business it's a constant war with competition to win business and grow market share. It's also a personal challenge to use all of this to focus inward and grow a business from nothing into a powerhouse that either makes a lot of money or is so effective that it is sold or acquired for a profit as well.

8. Understand the value of a strong peer network

In almost every case, entrepreneurs never get to success alone. The best understand it takes a network of contacts, business partners, financial partners, peers and resources to succeed. Effective people nurture these relationships and surround themselves with people who can help make them more effective. Any good leader is only as good as those who support him.

Assessment Functions with Opportunities

- The Challenge of New-Venture Start-ups.
- Pitfalls in Selecting New Ventures
- Critical Factors for New-Venture Development
- Why New Ventures Fail

- The Evaluation Process

1. Challenge of New- Venture Start-Ups
Need for:

- Approval
- Independence
- Personal Development

Also...

- Welfare (philanthropic) consideration
- Perception of wealth
- Tax reduction and indirect benefits

2. Pitfalls in Selecting New Ventures

- Lack of Objective Evaluation
- No Real Insight into the Market
- Inadequate Understanding of Technical Requirements
- Poor Financial Understanding
- Lack of Venture Uniqueness
- Ignorance of Legal Issues

3. Critical Factors for New Venture Development

- Uniqueness
- Investment
- Growth of Sales
- Product Availability
- Customer Availability

4. Why New Ventures Fail
Product/Market Problems:

- Poor timing
- Product design problems
- Inappropriate distribution strategy

- Unclear business definition
- Overreliance on one customer

Financial Difficulties:

- Initial undercapitalization
- Assuming debt too early
- Venture-capital relationship problems

Managerial Problems:

- Human Resource problems
- **Concept of a team approach**: Hiring and promotions Poor relationships Founder focused on weakness Incompetent support

5. The Evaluation Process

- Product Analysis
- Feasibility Criteria Approach
- **Comprehensive Feasibility:** Technical and Marketability

Marketing aspects of new ventures

Marketing Terms
   Market

- A group of consumers (potential customers) who have purchasing power and unsatisfied needs.
- A new venture will survive only if a market exists for its service.

Marketing Research

The gathering of information about a particular market, followed by an analysis of that information.
   Gathering Information
   Secondary Data

Information that has already been compiled.

- Advantage: Less expensive and available
- Disadvantages: outdated, lacks specificity, questionable validity
- Sources: internal and external sources

Primary Data
Information that is gathered specifically for the Research at hand.

- Surveys

- Experimentation

Developing an Information-Gathering Instrument

- Make sure each question pertains to a specific objective in line with the purpose of the study.
- Place simple questions first and difficult-to-answer questions later in the questionnaire.
- Ask: "How could this question be misinterpreted?" Reword questions to avoid misunderstanding.
- Avoid leading and biased questions.
- Give concise but not complete directions in the questionnaire.

Use scaled questions rather than simple yes/no Questions.
Interpreting and Reporting the Information
Data organized and analysed is information

- Tables, charts, graphs
- Descriptive statistics-mean, mode, median

Market research subject areas:

- Sales
- Distribution
- Markets
- Advertising
- Products

Inhibitors to Market Research and Reporting

Mistaken beliefs that inhibit the use of marketing research:

- **Cost:** Research is too expensive.
- **Complexity:** Research techniques rely on overly complex sampling, surveying, and statistical analysis.
- **Strategic Decisions:** Only major strategic decisions Need to be supported through marketing research.
- **Irrelevancy:** Research data will contain either information that merely supports what is already known or irrelevant information.

Internet Marketing

The Internet:

- Allows the firm to increase its presence and brand equity in the marketplace.
- Allows the company to cultivate new customers.
- Can improve customer service and lower costs by Allowing customers to serve themselves.
- Provides a mechanism for information sharing and Collection at a fraction of prior costs.
- Is a direct-sales distribution channel where the seller Buyer relationship is immediate, and the waiting

The period that follows a traditional marketing campaign is almost eliminated.

Developing the Market Concept

Market segmentation

1. The process of identifying a specific set of characteristics that differentiate one group of consumers from the rest.
2. Demographic variables: Age, material status, sex, occupation, income, location

3. Benefit variables: Convenience cost style trends depends on the nature of the particular new venture.

Consumer Behavior
The types and patterns of consumer characteristics.

- Personal Characteristics
- Psychological characteristics

Major Consumer Classifications

- Convenience goods
- Shopping goods
- Speciality goods
- Unsought goods
- New product

Developing a Marketing Plan
Marketing Planning

- The process of determining a clear, comprehensive approach to the creation of customers.

Elements of Marketing Planning > Current marketing research

- Current sales analysis
- Marketing information system
- Sales forecasting
- Evaluation

Current Marketing Research

- The purpose of marketing research is to identify Customers-target markets and to fulfil their desires.

Areas of Market Research

- The company's significant strengths and weaknesses

- Market profile
- Current and best customers
- Potential customers
- Competition
- Outside factors
- Legal changes

Business plan preparation for new ventures

The Importance of Planning

Planning is essential to the success of any undertaking. Critical factors that must be addressed when planning are:-

- **Realistic goals** – These must be specific, measurable, and set within time parameters.
- **Commitment** – The venture must be supported by all involved families, partners, employees, and team members.
- **Milestones** – Subgoals must be set for continual and timely evaluation of progress.
- **Flexibility** – Obstacles must be anticipated, and alternative strategies must be formulated.

Pitfalls to Avoid in Planning

- Pitfall 1: No Realistic Goals
- Pitfall 2: Failure to Anticipate Roadblocks
- Pitfall 3: No Commitment or Dedication
- Pitfall 4: Lack of Demonstrated Experience (Business or Technical)
- Pitfall 5: No Market Niche (Segment)

What is a Business Plan?

A written document that details the proposed venture:

- Describes the current status, expected needs, and projected results of the new business.

- Covers the project, marketing, research and development, manufacturing, management, critical risks, financing, and milestones or a timetable.
- Demonstrates a clear picture of what that venture is, where it is projected to go, and how the entrepreneur proposes it will get a there-a roadmap for a successful enterprise.

Benefits of a Business Plan
For the Entrepreneur:-

- The time, effort, research, and discipline required to create a formal business plan forces the entrepreneur to view operating strategies and expected results critically and objectively.

For Outside Evaluators:-

- The business plan provides a tool for use in Communications with outside financial sources.

Specifically for the Financial Sources:-

- Details the market potential and plans for securing a share of that market.
- Shows how the venture intends to service debt or provide an adequate return on equity.
- Identifies critical risks and crucial events with a discussion of contingency plans.
- Contains the necessary information for a thorough Business and financial evaluation.

Developing a Well-Conceived Business Plan
The Five-Minute Reading

- Determine the characteristics of the venture and its industry.
- Determine the financial structure of the plan (amount of debt or equity investment required).
- Read the latest balance sheet (to determine liquidity, net worth, and debt/equity).

- Determine the quality of entrepreneurs in the venture (sometimes the most crucial step).
- Establish the unique feature of this venture (find out what is Different).
- Read the entire plan over lightly (this is when the entire package is paged through for a casual look at graphs, charts, exhibits, and other plan components).

Guidelines to Remember

- Keep the plan respectably short
- Organize and package the plan appropriately
- Orient the plan toward the future
- Avoid exaggeration
- Highlight critical risks
- Give evidence of an effective entrepreneurial team
- Do not over-diversify · Identify the target market
- Keep the plan written in the third person
- Capture the reader's interest

Conclusion

A business plan conclusion is a summary of a business plan's strengths designed to convince the reader of the company's success. Because companies typically create business plans to get funding or investors, the conclusion should focus on how the organization makes money and why it is a good investment. Companies also make business plans to monitor their progress or set new goals.

The conclusion in a business plan is located either at the end of the document or at the end of the executive summary. The executive summary is an overview at the beginning of the business plan that tells the reader what they can expect to learn and convinces them to keep reading. Some people confuse the executive summary with the conclusion, but they differ in several important ways.

FOUR
INSTITUTIONS SUPPORTING SMALL BUSINESS ENTERPRISES

GOVERNMENT SUPPORT TO SMALL SCALE INDUSTRIES:-

Everything you need to know about the government support to small scale industries. The support system for small scale industries in India is quite comprehensive. Many of these agencies belong to the Central Government, while the rest belong to the state governments.

The small scale industry sector output contributes almost 40% of the gross industrial value-added, 45% of the total exports from India (direct as well as indirect exports) and is the second largest employer of human resources after agriculture.

The development of small scale sector has therefore been assigned an important role in India's national plans.

In order to protect, support, and promote small enterprises as also to help them become self-supporting, a number of protective and promotional measures have been undertaken by the government.

The various types of help extended by different support agencies of the government are:- 1. Credit Support 2. Marketing Support 3. Entrepreneurship Development 4. Technology Upgradation 5. Industrial Infrastructure 6. Technical Training 7. Institutional Structures 8. Assistance Programmes.

Government Support to Small Scale Industries – Central Government Agencies and State Government Agencies

The support system for SSI in India is quite comprehensive. Many of these agencies belong to the Central Government, while the rest belong to the state governments.

The small scale industry sector output contributes almost 40% of the gross industrial value-added, 45% of the total exports from India (direct as well as indirect exports) and is the second largest employer of human resources after agriculture. The development of small scale sector has therefore been assigned an important role in India's national plans.

GOVERNMENT SUPPORT TO SMALL SCALE INDUSTRIES: CREDIT SUPPORT, MARKETING SUPPORT, TECHNOLOGY UPGRADATION AND A FEW OTHERS:-

In order to protect, support, and promote small enterprises as also to help them become self-supporting, a number of protective and promotional measures have been undertaken by the government.

The promotional measures cover the following:

i. Industrial extension services,

ii. Institutional support in respect of credit facilities,

iii. Provision of developed sites for construction of sheds,

iv. Provision of training facilities,

v. Supply of machinery on hire-purchase terms,

vi. Assistance for domestic marketing as well as exports,

vii. Special incentive for setting up enterprises in backward areas, etc.

viii. Technical consultancy and financial assistance for technological up gradation.

While most of the institutional support services and some incentives are provided by the Central Government, others are offered by the state governments in varying degrees to attract investments and promote small industries in varying degrees to attract investments and promote small industries with a view to enhance industrial-production and to generate employment in their respective states.

Central-Level Institutions

1.Directorate of Industries (DI)

It involves in promotion of small-scale sectors at the state level.

2.DIC – District Industries Centre (DIC)

It promotes the development of Khadi and other village industries.

3. **Small Industries Development Organization (SIDO)**

It mainly acts as a nodal agency and an interface between central and state governments. It also gives wide ranging technical and consultancy services.

SIDO is created for development of various small-scale units in different areas. SIDO is a subordinate office of department of SSI and ARI. It is a nodal agency for identifying the needs of SSI units coordinating and monitoring the policies and programmes for promotion of the small industries. It undertakes various programmes of training, consultancy, evaluation for needs of SSI and development of industrial estates. All these functions are taken care with 27 offices, 31 SISI (Small Industries Service Institute) 31 extension centres of SISI and 7 centres related to production and process development. The activities of SIDO are divided into three categories as follows:

Coordination activities of SIDO:

- To coordinate various programmes and policies of various state governments pertaining to small industries.
- To maintain relation with central industry ministry, planning commission, state level industries ministry and financial institutions.
- Implement and coordinate in the development of industrial estates.
- Industrial development activities of SIDO:
- Develop import substitutions for components and products based on the data available for various volumes-wise and value-wise imports.
- To give essential support and guidance for the development of ancillary units.
- To provide guidance to SSI units in terms of costing market competition and to encourage them to participate in the government stores and purchase tenders.
- To recommend the central government for reserving certain items to
- produce at SSI level only.
- Management activities of SIDO:
- To provide training, development and consultancy services to SSI to develop their competitive strength.

4. **National Small Industries Corporation Ltd (NSIC)**

It is a Mini Ratna government agency established by the Ministry of Micro, Small and Medium Enterprises, Government of India in 1955. It has been working to promote, aid and foster the growth of micro, small and medium enterprises in the country.

5. **National Science and Technology Entrepreneurship Development Board (NSTEBDN)**

This agency promotes the usage of science and technology in SSI sectors.

6. **National Productivity Council (NPC)**

This agency suggests various ways of improving productivity.

7. **National Institute for small Industry Extension and Training (NIST)**

It imparts high-quality training to budding as well as existing entrepreneurs. It is in Hyderabad.

8. **National Institute for Entrepreneurship and Small Business Development (NIESBUD)**

It coordinates the efforts of various agencies involved in entrepreneurship development. It is in New Delhi.

9. **Indian Institute of Entrepreneurship (IIE)**

It aims to carry out research and development activities in entrepreneurship studies. It is located in Guwahati.

10. **Entrepreneurship Development Institute of India (EDII)**

It is an autonomous body sponsored by financial institutions like IDBI, ICICI etc. and engaged in spearheading and inspiring entrepreneurship movements in India. It is in Ahmedabad.

State-Level Institutions

1.Small Scale Industries Board (SSI BOARD)

It is the apex advisory body to the central Government in matters related to the small-scale sectors in the country.

2. Khadi and Village Industries Commission (KVIC)

It is a statutory body formed in April 1957 by the Government of India, under the act of Parliament, 'Khadi and Village Industries Commission Act of 1956. Its purpose is to plan, promote, organise and assist in the establishment and development of Khadi and Village Industries.

3. State Financial Corporation (SFC)

It provides financial support for starting SSIs. It helps in ensuring balanced regional development, higher investment, more employment generation and broad ownership of various industries.

4. SIDC: State Industrial Development Corporation (SIDC)

It promotes infrastructure facilities. It also procures scarce raw materials from the domestic market and makes them available to needy small-scale industries as per their requirements.

5. SSIDC: State Small Industrial Development Corporation (SSIDC)

It helps small and tiny units in the procurement of scarce raw materials. It also gives other services.

4.3 Other Agencies

There are a number of other agencies both central and state level- that directly or indirectly help the cause of the small-scale sector in India, mainly in the financial and industrial domain. They are:

1. Small Industries Development Bank of India (SIDBI)

The small Industries and Development Bank of India (SIDBI) is a regulatory body for licensing and regulation of MSMEs. SIDBI's primary objective is to help banks in assisting MSMEs and SSIs to get funds for business expansion purposes and to meet working capital requirements.

2. National Bank for Agricultural and Rural Development (NABARD)

National Bank for Agriculture and Rural Development or NABARD is the main regulatory body in the country's rural banking system and is considered the peak development finance institution which is established and owned by the government of India. This bank aims to provide and regulate credit to rural areas, which will be the first step towards enhancing rural development in the country.

3. Housing and Urban Development Corporation Ltd. (HUDCO)

HUDCO stands for Housing and Urban Development Corporation Limited. It a wholly-owned government company which provides loans for housing and urban infrastructure projects in India. Its vision is to become a leading techno-financial institution to promote sustainable habitat development for transforming the lives of people.

4. Non-governmental Organizations (NGOs)

A non-governmental organization (NGO) is a non-profit group that functions independently of any government. NGOs, sometimes called civil societies, are organized on community, national and international levels to serve a social or political goal such as humanitarian causes or the environment.

5. Export Promotion Council (EPC)

Export Promotion Councils are government-initiated authorities that promote and support export firms in developing their overseas trade and presence by providing technical and industry insights. Additionally, EPCs also promote government schemes, act as a data store and conduct overseas tours and studies. They also act as an intermediary between the government and the export industry and are critical in formulating the foreign policies of the country.

6. Confederation of Indian Industries (CII)

The Confederation of Indian Industry (CII) works to create and sustain an environment conducive to the development of India, partnering with Industry, Government and civil society, through advisory and consultative processes.

CII is a non-government, not-for-profit, industry-led and industry-managed organization, with around 9000 members from the private as well as public sectors, including SMEs and MNCs, and an indirect membership of over 300,000 enterprises from 286 national and regional sectoral industry bodies.

7. Federation of Indian Chambers of Commerce and Industry (FICCI)

FICCI provides reports, in-depth research papers, surveys and analyses of all sectors of the global economy. Every year, the company organises around 300 conferences and summits each year and is one of the leading providers of trade fairs and exhibitions. The company was established in 1977 and is based in India.

8. Associated Chamber of Commerce and Industry of India (ASSOCHAM)

ASSOCHAM is authorised by the Government of India to issue Certificates of Origin, certify commercial invoices, and recommend business visas.

9. World Association for Small and Medium Enterprises (WASME)

The objectives of WASME for the growth and promotion of Micro organizations and MSMEs are as follows. - Articulating concerns and interests of MSMEs at various UN and international fora, Networking with related/similar organisations and Capacity building of MSMEs through managerial and skill development programmes.

10. Indian Council of Small Industries (ICSI)

Indian Council of Small Industries is a non-profit organisation, established in 1987 that works primarily in the domain of Education and Technology. Its primary office is in Kolkata, West Bengal.

Conclusion

Central-level institutions are developed by the Government of India at central and state levels. Some of the central-level institutions include DI, DIC, SIDO, NSIC, NPC etc.

The State level institutions comprise SSI Board, KVIC, SFC, SSIDC etc.

There are a number of other agencies both central and state levels- that directly or indirectly help the cause of the small-scale sector in India, mainly in the financial and industrial domains. They are SIDBI, NABARD SIDCO, NGO etc.

4.4 Industry Associations

An industry association is an organization that supports companies and employers of a particular type of industry and protects their rights.

Industry associations play a critical role in **establishing a bridge between the industry and the government**. Besides, they also work for the industry's interests by imparting education, formulating technical standards, conducting surveys, helping to penetrate export markets, etc.

The stages of establishing a new association are:

- Research your market well.
- Design the services that will be offered to potential members.
- Agree on the subscription scales.
- Develop a marketing strategy.
- Maintain momentum.

Industry associations may:

- Give you information about your industry (i.e., how changes to legislation will affect your business)
- Provide you with useful resources (i.e., information and programs to help you meet industry standards)
- Run training and education programs
- Organise seminars
- Facilitate networking events
- Manage mentoring programs
- Connect you with other businesses in your industry
- Arrange public relations or advertising activities to promote your industry
- Organise advertising campaigns to educate or persuade the public about issues relevant to your industry
- Lobby on behalf of your industry to influence government policy.

These associations offer some information and services for free, but, in most cases, you need to become a member and pay a fee to access their full range of information, resources and services.

In many industries, becoming a member of the peak body can give your business credibility as your membership proves to customers that you have met strict criteria and have certain qualifications and experience.

Trade Associations

A trade association is a voluntary organization of independent business units in the same branch of industry, which conducts co-operatively activities aimed at improving the welfare of the group, which does not deprive its members of the power to make essential managerial decisions.

The meetings of the trade associations generally discuss issues relating to the common interest of the members. Issues may relate to:

- Taxation (tax rates and taxation procedures)
- Raw material prices or shortages
- Infrastructural issues (roads, power, telecom, ports etc.)
- Labour issues and labour legislation
- Legislation affecting the interests of the members
- Unfair competition
- Import and export issues
- Emerging opportunities in business, trade and commerce

Features of Trade associations

1. **Voluntary association** – It is a voluntary association of member units. Members are free to exit at any time.
2. **Non-profit motive** – Trade associations are non-profit earning associations. They are not promoted with a commercial motive.
3. **Name** – The associations are generally named after the nature of the trade or industry conducted by its members.
4. **Identity** – Members continue to retain their individual identities.
5. **Independence** – Members' units can remain completely independent. There is no interference by the association on the business affairs of its members.

6. **Objective** – The objective of trade associations is to promote the business interests of the members, exchange views, serve as a platform for discussions and represent the interests of its members.

Conclusion

An industry association is an organisation that supports companies and employers of a particular type of industry and protects their rights. It offers some information and services for free but in most cases, you need to become a member and pay a fee to access information, services etc. Its features are a voluntary association, non-profit motive, name, identity, independence and objective.

FIVE

DISCUSSION ON CURRENT GOVERNMENT SCHEMES SUPPORTING ENTREPRENEURSHIP AN FINDING OUT WHICH SCHEME WILL MOST SUIT THE BUSINESS PLAN

Government Schemes in India are launched by the government to address the social and economic welfare of the citizens of this nation.

These schemes play a crucial role in solving many socio-economic problems that beset Indian society, and thus their awareness is a must for any concerned citizen.

On February 1, 2021, the Finance Minister of India released the Union Budget 2021-22 and made new announcements regarding the government schemes in India. In 2020, a relief package worth Rs 1.70 lakh crore was announced to tackle the financial difficulties which were faced due to the COVID-19 outbreak under the PM Garib Kalyan Yojana. This year, the government has announced the Aatmanirbhar package amounting to Rs. 27.1 lakh crores to deal with the impact of coronavirus.

This article will provide all the details of the Government Schemes 2022 that are implemented in India.

- **About the Government Schemes:-**

Knowing all the government schemes is one thing, but the candidates must also know their purpose. Candidates stand a better chance of scoring high marks if and when they go through the purpose of each scheme given below.

1. Pradhan Mantri Jan Dhan Yojana: Pradhan Mantri Jan Dhan Yojana is a National Mission on Financial Inclusion that provides an integrated approach to bring about robust financial inclusion and ultimately provide banking services to all households in the country.

2. Make in India: PM Narendra Modi launched the 'Make in India' campaign that will facilitate investment, foster innovation, enhance protection for intellectual property and build best in manufacturing infrastructure.

'Make in India' has identified 25 sectors in manufacturing, infrastructure and service activities and detailed information is being shared through interactive web-portal and professionally developed brochures.

3. Swachh Bharat Mission: Swachh Bharat Mission was launched in the entire country as a national movement. The campaign aims to achieve the vision of a 'Clean India' by 2nd October 2019. The Swachh Bharat Abhiyan is the most significant campaign with regard to sanitation by the Government of India.

4. Beti Bachao Beti Padhao: The goal of this scheme is to make girls socially and financially self-reliant through education.

5. Atal Pension Yojna: Atal Pension Yojana is a pension scheme mainly aimed at providing a universal pension scheme for those who are a part of the unorganized sector such as maids, gardeners, delivery boys, etc. This scheme replaced the previous Swavalamban Yojana which wasn't well-received by the people.

6. Digital India Mission: The Digital India programme is a flagship programme of the Government of India with a vision to transform India into a digitally empowered society and knowledge economy.

7. Pradhan Mantri Shram Yogi Maan-dhan: It is a voluntary and contributory pension scheme, under which the subscriber would receive the following benefits:

(i) Minimum Assured Pension: Each subscriber under the PM-SYM, shall receive a minimum assured pension of Rs 3000/- per month after attaining the age of 60 years.

(ii) Family Pension: During the receipt of a pension, if the subscriber dies, the spouse of the beneficiary shall be entitled to receive 50% of the pension received by the beneficiary as a family pension. Family pension is applicable only to a spouse.

(iii) If a beneficiary has given a regular contribution and died due to any cause (before age of 60 years), his/her spouse will be entitled to join and continue the scheme subsequently by payment of regular contribution or exit the scheme as per provisions of exit and withdrawal.

8. Gold Monetisation Scheme: Gold Monetisation Scheme was launched by the Government of India in 2015, under this scheme one can deposit their gold in any form in a GMS account to earn interest as the price of the gold metal goes up.

9. PM CARES Fund -Prime Minister's Citizen Assistance and Relief in Emergency Situation Fund: This is a public charitable trust initiated by Prime Minister Narendra Modi. This national trust is created with the objective to meet the distressed and dreadful situations like COVID-19 in the times ahead. PM CARES was initiated on March 28, 2020, under the chairmanship of the Indian Prime Minister with the Ministry of Home Affairs, Defence Minister and Finance Minister as the ex-officio Trustee.

10. Aarogya Setu: The Government of India took the initiative to fight the Coronavirus pandemic. It launched a mobile application to spread the awareness of COVID_19 among the citizens of India through an app called Aarogya Setu. The Aarogya Setu mobile app has been developed by the National Informatics Centre (NIC) that comes under the Ministry of Electronics and Information Technology. For detailed information, visit the link of Aarogya Setu given above.

11. Ayushman Bharat: Launched in 2018 by Prime Minister Narendra Modi Ayushman Bharat is a health scheme. It is the largest government-funded healthcare programme in the world with over 50 crore beneficiaries. The Ayushman Bharath programme has two sub-missions PM-JAY & HWCs.

- Pradhan Mantri Jan Arogya Yojana (PM-JAY), earlier known as the National Health Protection Scheme (NHPS) will cover the financial protection for availing healthcare services at the secondary and tertiary levels.
- Health and Wellness Centres (HWCs) are aimed at improving access to cheap and quality healthcare services at the primary level. Read about Ayushman Bharat in detail in the link provided above.

12. UMANG – Unified Mobile Application for New-age Governance is a mobile application launched by PM Narendra Modi to provide secured access to the citizens to multiple government services at one platform. UMANG is a key component of the Digital India initiative of the government that intends to make all traditional offline government services available 24 * 7 online through a single unified app.

References

1. https://www.investopedia.com/terms/e/entrepreneur.asp
2. https://www.gbslepgrowthhub.co.uk/news/5-benefits-of-entrepreneurship-in-the-economy
3. https://www.toppr.com/guides/business-studies/small-business/roles-of-small-businesses-in-india-and-problems-of-small-businesses/
4. https://businessconnectindia.in/patricia-narayan/,https://www.yosuccess.com/success-stories/patricia-narayan-success-story/
5. https://www.indiatimes.com/trending/human-interest/success-story-of-karsanbhai-patel-543621.html#highlight_54306
6. https://www.ciim.in/ramesh-babu-barber-owns-rolls-royce-motivation-story/
7. https://www.slideshare.net/kunaldrizzy/creativity-and-innovation-in-entrepreneurship
8. https://www.entrepreneur.com/article/277379
9. https://www.inventiva.co.in/stories/legal-challenges-faced-by-the-start-ups-in-india/
10. https://www.ey.com/en_nl/finance-navigator/12-sources-of-finance-for-entrepreneurs-make-sure-you-pick-the-right-one
11. https://www.investopedia.com/terms/e/entrepreneur.asp
12. https://www.gbslepgrowthhub.co.uk/news/5-benefits-of-entrepreneurship-in-the-economy
13. https://byjus.com/commerce/meaning-nature-and-types-of-small-business/
14. https://courses.lumenlearning.com/ivytech-introbusiness/chapter/reading-advantages-and-disadvantages-of-small-business-
15. https://www.toppr.com/guides/business-studies/small-business/roles-of-small-businesses-in-india-and-problems-of-small-businesses/
16. https://businessconnectindia.in/patricia-narayan/, https://www.yosuccess.com/success-stories/patricia-narayan-success-story/
17. https://www.indiatimes.com/trending/human-interest/success-story-of-karsanbhai-patel-543621.html#highlight_54306
18. https://www.ciim.in/ramesh-babu-barber-owns-rolls-royce-motivation-

story/
19. https://www.citehr.com/20902-story-dhirubhai-ambani.html
20. https://www.whizsky.com/kailash-katkar-early-life-struggle-and-an-ultimate-success-story/
21. https://www.slideshare.net/kunaldrizzy/creativity-and-innovation-in-entrepreneurship
22. https://www.entrepreneur.com/article/277379
23. https://www.inventiva.co.in/stories/legal-challenges-faced-by-the-start-ups-in-india/
24. https://www.ey.com/en_nl/finance-navigator/12-sources-of-finance-for-entrepreneurs-make-sure-you-pick-the-right-one
25. https://www.slideshare.net/drumacasieb/assessment-of-entrepreneurial-opportunities
26. https://slideplayer.com/slide/12645971/
27. https://slideplayer.com/slide/13655096/
28. https://www.scribd.com/presentation/432519165/Central-and-State-Level-Financial-Institutions
29. https://www.business.qld.gov.au/starting-business/planning/market-customer-research/resources/associations
30. https://accountlearning.com/trade-associations-definition-features-functions-advantages/